CREATE A COURSE IN 28 DAYS

A SIMPLE GUIDE TO HOSTING YOUR FIRST PROFITABLE ONLINE PROGRAM

CW00828394

Jeannie Sullivan

Stoney Point Press

Chapin, SC

Stoney Point Press
124 Stoney Point Lane
Chapin, SC 29036

Ordering Information:
Quantity sales. Special discounts are available on quantity purchases by corporations, associations, and others. For details, contact the "Special Sales Department" at the address above.

Create a Course in 28 Days / Jeannie Sullivan. —1st ed.

ISBN (paperback) 978-1-7360381-0-9

CONTENTS

This book is dedicated to you, my courageous reader.
The world needs your course.

Dream, Then Do

What if you decided that starting today, it all changes.
No more small-time
No more bashfulness
No more wondering, waiting, wishing, or wanting.

Just dream, then do.

Or if you're still searching for your dream, just do.
Do what feels light or
Just do what makes you feel.

Because feeling anything at all will open you up,
Throw you down, and then release you
From all that you thought you knew;
All that you thought you couldn't change;

All that you created while on autopilot -
Never realizing the mystery is solved inside you
Waiting on you to align to something bigger,
Bigger than you could ever even imagine
Because that is what you were born for...

Dream, then do.

INTRODUCTION

I felt guilty.

All my life, I thought I was a terrible procrastinator. Once in college, I tried doing things the "right" way. I went to the library early. Created an outline. Wrote a first and second draft. I made a C. After that, I didn't understand why my process worked, but I honored it. I wrote my papers the night before they were due. I made A's.

And I rarely told anyone. It felt like cheating. Years later, Gretchen Rubin's book, *Better than Before*, changed my life.

I am a sprinter.

The pressure of a deadline creates clarity. I put the assignment in my head long before I start putting anything on paper. My ideas come together while I'm doing other things. When the time comes, the final product spills out in record time, like magic.

This epiphany changed the way I work with course creators. Many of them come to me with a brilliant idea. Yet, they can't seem to get their lessons finished, despite their commitment and passion. They thrive on the exchange of ideas and energy to guide their words and inspire their message.

In the traditional course creation process, this gets lost.

That's why I wrote this book.

To offer you a different path. Because I know you've grown weary. Like when I wrote that paper in college, you followed the steps in perfect order: Design a funnel. Create some pre-recorded modules. Put them online. Wake up to registrations.

But that's not quite happening yet, is it? As entrepreneurs, we've spent a lot of years mistaking information for learning. One of my all-time favorite quotes comes from the author, Leo Buscaglia:

"Change is the result of all true learning."

Information alone does not equal learning. Watching a video does not equal learning. Learning happens when you apply new concepts and experience a result. Learning requires action and feedback loops.

Those of us participating in online education are requiring more. We're seeking a transformation. And we need teachers, experts, luminaries - like you - to take us by the hand and show us a direct path to results. If you can deliver on your promise, we are eager to invest. That's the power of learning-based revenue.

Take a moment now to reflect. Because I bet if you're reading this book, you're not only a natural teacher but a lifelong learner. What is the best online course you've ever paid for and completed? Keep thinking. Keep going. I know it's a long list but dig deep. Is there an online course you've taken that's changed your life in some way?

Yes. I thought you'd had at least one great experience with an online program, or you wouldn't have picked up this book.

Just imagine: You now have everything you need to create that kind of impact on other people's lives.

Let me share a little story with you. In many ways, I've been writing this book for the last 12 years. It was 2009, and I was attending an online coach certification program. Now, this was before Zoom, and video conferencing was still a luxury most of us had never experienced. So night after night, I put my kids to bed and dialed into my classes. People from all over the world gathered for these classes. We learned how to help people create their lives.

Almost daily, I heard aspiring coaches talking about how they wanted to offer group programs. Then, transition participants into individual clients if it was a good fit. Then one night after I got off these calls, I had an idea: What if I could use my background in Learning and Development to guide my classmates through creating their workshops?

Being a sprinter, I created the course outline and flyer right away. Posted it on the school's electronic bulletin board (it's 2009, remember?). I charged a small fee of $25 per person for my first paid online program: Create a Coaching Workshop in 4 Weeks.

The course was full by the time I woke up the next morning. This was my first taste of learning-based revenue. And it's where the process I'm teaching you in this book was born.

This year, I've heard from two coaches who attended that original class. Both of them shared that they've been using the tools I taught them for the last 10 years. One of them now runs a coaching certification program of her own.

In this book, I share a refined version of the process I taught in that very first class. If you follow the steps here, you'll create an online program that achieves measurable results and leads you to profitability in just 28 days.

Let me be clear – if you're looking for a detailed process that contains scripts and prescribes a fail-proof technique to earn six figures by the end of the year - this book is NOT for you.

On the contrary...

If you thrive under pressure, appreciate simplicity, and trust the process - this book is for you.

If you're a little bit scrappy, have fun learning new technology, and are willing to take a risk - this book is for you.

If you've tried traditional course creation processes in the past but never quite cross the finish line - this book is for you.

If you feel that somewhere deep inside you, there's a course waiting to be born - this book is for you.

If you feel that the lessons you've learned the hard way can help others, this book is for you.

If you're a little bit scared and entirely overwhelmed by searching "Create an Online Course" in Google - this book is for you.

If you're interested in adding a revenue stream to your life that is also fun and makes a difference in the world - this book is for you.

Your adventures in course creation are waiting. Let's go.

You've got this.

Think of this book as the Couch to 5K for creating a course. Are you familiar with the C25K program? I've completed it twice in the last two decades and started it about 10 more times. But I keep going back to it again and again. Because it works, as long as I'm willing to complete the steps. The steps are clear and easy to follow: walk 5 minutes, run 90 seconds, walk 3 minutes, etc. I really enjoy that I don't have to be the one to make the plan. I can just put on my running shoes and hit play on the app.

That's how I've written this book. If you complete the steps, you'll be ready to host a proven online program that will be profitable from the beginning. Sound good? Yep! I thought it might. However, like the C25K program, it only works if you complete the steps.

Each day, I'll provide a little context and a daily task. My goal is to keep these tasks to about 30 minutes each. But some may take you longer. It all depends on how much time you invest. I'd like to encourage you to follow this piece of advice I got from a manager very early on in my instructional design career: Done is better than perfect. So the first time you're going through this process, here's what I recommend:

1. Read your daily task.
2. Gather any tools you need to complete the task.
3. Set a timer for 30 minutes. Do as much as you can on the task - working quickly.
4. Walk away when the timer goes off.
5. Revisit the task later in the day and ask: "What else needs to be done here to call it 80% complete?"

Psst! If you'd like to access free tutorials and handouts to help with your course creation, you can download them here: jeanniesullivan.com/28days

Find your perfect topic.

She said, "I've thought about creating an online course, but I have no idea what my topic would be." We were only 15 minutes into our first conversation. I already had three ideas to offer. I can't help it! It's how my brain works. And I've learned to ask permission: "Would you mind if I share some ideas with you?" This happens when I talk to experts, like you, about creating online group programs. It's hard for you to imagine what would be relevant or meaningful in a short course because you know every detail. Yet, your learners are starting at the beginning.

Why not create a course that establishes a foundation or prepares them for what's next? That way, if they choose to continue working with you 1:1 or in another group program, they are ready to receive the transformation you have to offer them.

Today's task is to find your perfect (and most profitable!) topic. Here are three questions to get you started:

- What information do you share over and over again on client calls?
- What foundational or introductory learning experience could you provide for new clients who are just getting started in your area of expertise?
- What are your clients always asking for help with that you don't currently offer in your services?

Once you've answered these questions, you should have a list of at least 5 topics for your course. Now, as you review your plan, I can hear the "yeah, but" rolling around in your head. "Yeah, but there are already tons of courses and resources available on the topic I'd like to teach."

So, I hope you'll indulge me by quickly answering these questions. Just an estimated guess for each one will do fine.

How many books on leadership have you read?
How many marketing podcasts have you listened to?
How many free downloads do you currently have in your folder?

I'm willing to bet that the ideas you learned about when you read, listened, or downloaded these resources aren't original. It's the words a thought leader uses to grab your attention in a new way. It's the story the creator shares that finally hits home for you. It's the question you've heard countless times before, but for some reason - no one knows why, and it doesn't really matter - today is the first day you stopped to truly consider your answer. And like magic, your belief suddenly shifts, and you feel inspired to take action instead of holding back.

That's what you have the opportunity to provide for learners in your course. Even if there are already 11,234 courses on the same topic.

DAY ONE TASK

Select three topics for your course that you are most excited about.

For each one, answer the questions below:

- What will your learners be able to do after your class that they couldn't do before? (The goal is transformation, not information sharing.)

- Describe the audience for your course. Do your participants have the resources to be able to purchase your program? (This guide is designed for profitable programs.)

- What excites you most about teaching this course? (If you're not excited about your topic, it's going to be a L-O-N-G 28 days!)

- How does this topic relate to your existing business? (I advise you to choose a topic that won't require you to cultivate an entirely new set of prospects.)

- Can this topic be taught in three hours or less? (If so, it's an excellent fit for this program! If not, keep looking for a more specific topic.)

Do you have a clear winner? Great! If not, don't worry. Tuck your analysis away and take a fresh look in the morning.

Pro tip: Don't move on to Day 2 until you've decided on your topic.

What's your perfect course topic?
And what makes this one your best fit for profitability right now?

Meet your ideal learner.

It was several years ago now when my son turned to me and said, "Mom, I don't understand your job at all." At the time, I was working on a large mobile learning project for a major tire manufacturer. He'd overheard one of my calls in the car that day. "You don't know anything about cars, much less tires. How in the world can you create training on them?"

I explained that my lack of expertise makes me the perfect person for the job. Experts forget what it's like to not yet know what they know. Because of this, it's tough for an expert to teach a beginner. They leave out the essential steps of the process. They tend to overestimate a base level of knowledge.

As an instructional designer, I step in and play the role of the learner. I ask questions from a beginner's point of view. Because you're the expert and the instructional designer in the course creation process, it's time to ask yourself some questions to bring you back to a beginner's state of mind.

DAY TWO TASK

Set a timer for 25 minutes and explore the world of your ideal learner. If you need a few questions to get you started, try these:

- What are their biggest dreams that they've rarely shared with anyone?
- What are they afraid of?
- How have they tried to learn about your topic in the past?
- What are their most significant barriers to reaching their goal?
- How will their lives be different after completing your course?
- Where will they get the funding to learn from you?
- When will they fit the coursework into their daily life?
- Where do they gather online when they aren't in your course?

Now, look at your answers and make a list of 5-10 ideal learners who are already in your network. These may be people who were interested in your individual services but didn't have the budget. They might have shown interest in your services, but the timing wasn't quite right.

Make the list below and set it aside for later in our process.

Play with the numbers.

If you are interested in figuring out how a learning-based revenue stream can support your business, calculate your ROI. What is ROI? It stands for Return on Investment. Going through this process now will prepare you to make important pricing decisions later.

Here is a simple equation for calculating the ROI: ROI = [(Payback - Investment)/Investment)] x 100

Your payback is the total amount of money earned from your course. Investment relates to the amount of resources put into creating your course. To calculate the ROI for your learning programs, first identify the following targets:

- What will you charge as the registration fee?
- How many participants would you like to have?
- What are the total costs for the creation and administration of your program?

If you're not sure how much to include for video conferencing and email marketing tools, add about $50 per month for now.

For example: A coach is offering an online course to 10 participants at a registration fee of $249. The investment of webinar hosting and email marketing is $64/month. The online course is offered monthly.

Payback = 10 participants x $249 registration fee = $2,490
ROI = [(Payback - Investment)/Investment)] x 100
ROI = [($2,490 - $65)/$65] x 100

ROI = [$2,425/$65] x 100
ROI = [37.31] x 100 = 3,730%

In this example, the return on investment is 3,730% - WOW! That's a massive return on investment! One thing we haven't considered yet is the time investment in the process. If you are interested in factoring in your time investment, consider these two questions:

- How many hours will you spend preparing for and facilitating your course?
- What is the hourly value of your time?

Let's look at the same example considering time investment: The time spent will be 10 hours (on average per month), and the hourly value is $45/hour. I will multiply these and add them to the investment.

Investment = (10 hours x $45 hourly value) + $65 costs = $515
ROI = [($2,490 - $515)/$515] x 100
ROI = [$1,975/$515] x 100
ROI = [3.83] x 100 = 383%

Adding In your time Investment really changes the equation! Keep in mind that 100% ROI means that you completely recouped your investment. Anything over 100% means you are making money!

Use the formulas and play with the numbers. Then, notice how you're feeling about them.

Payback = # participants _____ x registration fee _____ = $_____

Investment = (# hours _____ x hourly value $_____) + costs $_____

ROI = [(Payback $_____ - Investment $_____)/Investment $_____] x 100

What is your ROI? _____

Once you calculate ROI, you may want to adjust the variable to create a more profitable opportunity. Try increasing your registration fee or the number of participants to find a worthwhile balance and a reasonable investment for your participants.

Remember that you may have one-time investment costs to get your program created and running smoothly. Then, you'll be able to enjoy an ongoing learning-based revenue stream.

Here's the sweet spot I recommend for your first course: Find the number that generates these two feelings: You are confident that any learner will be overjoyed with the value they get from your course for the price they paid. You will be thrilled with the profit you receive to create and host your first profitable online program.

When both are true, you've hit the right number.

Try this:
As you adjust the number of participants and your course price, notice the feelings you have. Are you getting excited? Nervous? Make some notes below.

Discover your course creation style.

Knowing your preferences for designing content is essential to completing your course development. Not all creatives approach a project similarly, with the same tools, or the same thought processes. In my work with course designers, I've come to recognize three distinct styles of creation.

Focused Finisher

Loves a project plan, checklists, and completing tasks. Dives into new technology without hesitation and is a self-starter. Focused Finishers are detail-oriented, thrive on completing tasks, explore new technology with ease, and tend to be self-starters. Focused Finishers know who they are. And If you're not a Focused Finisher, you've probably had moments (like I have!) when you wished you were one. If this isn't you, don't worry. Keep reading.

Mixed Media Maverick

Gets excited about learning new tools and technology but also enjoys connecting with small groups of people. These creators can follow a schedule and project plan pretty well, but also enjoy coloring outside the lines. Mixed Media Mavericks seek out new tools, love connecting with others online, and don't shy away from project plans. They are quick to innovate and try new ways of getting things done.

Workshop Wonder

Shines in front of a classroom, whether it's online or in-person. These natural facilitators love to be "in the flow" of exchanging ideas. Workshop Wonders thrive in live workshops, tend to love teaching, and can typically walk into a room with little or no preparation without skipping a beat.

Course creation processes that require detailed scripts and step-by-step tutorials can be tedious for Workshop Wonders. But don't fret, that's not what we are doing here.

Need a little guidance? Take my online quiz to find your style here: jeanniesullivan.com/style

Knowing your Course Creation Style comes in handy when you're determining the digital format for your course. Take a few minutes to read through the table below and choose a format for the course you're creating through the process in this book.

Psst! Don't worry, you can always change this choice later. Remember, done is better than perfect.

DAY FOUR TASK

Determine your Course Creation Style and select a format for your course.

Live, Online Series	Perfect for Workshop Wonders + Mixed Media Mavericks Rapid Development Process Great for Testing Ideas	If the thought of sitting down to write scripts and create tons of worksheets makes you run and hide, this strategy will likely become your go-to model. It's one of the best options for piloting your program and getting measurable outcomes quickly.
Live, Online Workshop	An expedited version of the live, online series Perfect for Workshop Wonders	If your program outcomes can be realized within a half-day or full day, this is a great option. Gather your learners online for a fully interactive session that combines presentations or teaching segments and co-working sessions.
Digital Evergreen	An excellent option for Focused Finishers Typically sold at a lower price Closest to passive revenue	A digital evergreen program is the closest of all the online course formats to passive revenue. Typically, these programs are sold directly through ads or an email sales sequence for less than $200. However, completion rates tend to be lower than any of the other formats.
Digital + Accelerator	Increases Engagement and Completion Rates Blended Learning Approach Adds Live, Online Sessions to Evergreen Program	Adding an accelerator to your digital evergreen program increases engagement, boost completion rates, and creates raving fans. While your content is still delivered digitally, you show up live with your learners in a group format. This generates excitement and creates accountability.

Gain a little clarity.

First of all, let's celebrate! You have done the work to start seeing your program come together! Our next step in the course creation process is critical to your success. It's the course clarity statement. Your course clarity statement is like your elevator pitch for your program. When you are clear about who your course helps, what It helps them do, and how It makes their lives better - everything flows.

Here's the formula for your course clarity statement:

My course helps (target audience) learn how to (result) so they can (benefit).

My example:

My course helps experts and entrepreneurs learn how to create profitable courses that inspire real transformation, so they create learning-based revenue and feel great about making a lasting impact on their learners' lives.

Another example:

My course helps aspiring wedding planners learn how to launch a successful business so they can earn money doing the work they've been dreaming of for years.

DAY FIVE TASK

Write your course clarity statement. Then put it away and review it again later in the day.

My course helps (<u>target audience</u>) learn how to (<u>result</u>) so they can (<u>benefit</u>).

Try it out on your mom, your best friend, your dog, and maybe even a couple of strangers.

- Do they clearly understand what your course is about from this one statement?
- Do they understand who the course is for?
- Are they clear on the transformation that participants will create in their lives?
- Do they clearly understand why someone would want to take your course?

If the answer is yes to all of the above, you've done it! You're ready for Day 6.

Map your learner's transformation.

"How many videos do I have to include in my online course?" I get this question at least once a week. And my answer is never popular: it depends. When people register for your course, it's not because they need more information. Creators upload more than 4 million hours of content to YouTube every single day.

Your participants are not looking for information; they are looking for an expert:

- a guide who has already sorted through the content
- a teacher who has carved out a direct path to the transformation they are seeking

A new entrepreneur doesn't sign up for your program to learn about selling. She wants to increase her sales. If you can help her do that in the next 7 days, even better.

An aspiring flower farmer doesn't register for your course to learn about flowers. She wants to grow a garden. If you can help her plant a seed in the first 30 minutes, you've created a priceless program.

It's the results you deliver that determine the value of your program. It makes no difference how many videos, worksheets, or downloads you create.

DAY SIX TASK

Now, we're going to identify your learner's transformation target. First, answer this question: By the end of my program, what will learners do that they couldn't do before taking your program?

Sample Transformation Target

After completing my program, participants will know how to start their own wedding planning business. (This example comes from Jessica Rourke, creator of *Engage: A Business Blueprint for Wedding Planners*.)

Here's a table to help you map your learners' journey through the transformation.

1. In the first column, describe where your learner is when they start your program.
2. In the third column, answer a slightly different set of questions that will reflect where your learner is at the end of your program.
3. Then add three steps in the middle column that reflect your genius and will become the signature process for this course.

Before	Your Signature Process	After
What do they know? What do they not know? What frustrations are they experiencing?		What do they now know? What do they still have to learn? What aspirations have they achieved?

Yes! Complete the first and third columns first. Then go to the middle column and list three essential steps that your learner will complete to get from point A to point B. This becomes your signature process for your course. You must stick to three actions if you plan to finish your project in 28 days.

It will probably be tough to keep the list to 3 steps, but it's super important that you follow this guideline. If you find yourself with a list of more than 3, ask yourself these questions to narrow the list:

- Is this step essential to achieving their transformation target?
- Is there a way to integrate this step into one of the others?
- If this topic isn't covered, will my learners still succeed?

Now that you've got a list of your 3 signature steps, it's time to build upon them to create real transformation. See, what sets a learning program apart from a product is a design that inspires lasting change.

Write your three signature steps below.

Design a compelling learning sequence.

If you want to be a great teacher, stop sharing so much information. Because you're the expert, it's hard. The course you're creating is for people just starting to do what you've mastered over your career. Your job as a course creator is to deconstruct your zone of genius step by step.

And it's not easy. It takes courage to look at your work from a new perspective.

I remember a story that one of my professors shared in my graduate classes. Imagine it's your first day in a photography class. You've got your camera. And you've finally committed to taking your passion for photography one step further.

The teacher shows up and dives into a long history of digital photography. You try to stay awake but your eyes keep rolling back in your head.

What do you really want to do on your first day?

Yes! Take a picture!

Your learners seek a direct path to the transformation that inspired them to show up and invest in your program. That's where compelling learning sequences come in: they are specifically designed to guide your learner directly to the action they must take to create the transformation they seek.

Each of your signature steps (see Day 6) requires a compelling learning sequence.

A compelling learning sequence is a simple process to guide participants to take action and achieve measurable results from your program. Each sequence is made up of seven content areas designed to support each of your signature process steps.

Curiosity: Share a story, ask a question, present a statistic or share a quote that will ignite curiosity.

Understanding: What facts, concepts, or processes does your learner need to understand to take the action required for this step.

Action: One of the steps from your signature process goes here.

Resistance: Ask yourself, "What are the 'yeah, buts' that my learner is thinking at this point in time?" Really put yourself in the learner's shoes and directly address each area of resistance you encounter.

Vision: Remind them of their "why." Ask them a question that will bring them back to the feeling of having accomplished their goal.

Evaluation: Clarify what success looks like. Recap the action required in this step. (This is an excellent time for a "done is better than perfect" message.)

Encouragement: Remind participants that you've given them everything they need to succeed. Recap the action and the support you've provided your learners. A quick "I believe in you!" can work wonders here.

Draft a compelling learning sequence for the first step in your signature process.

It might help to create a simple table like the one below to help you organize your thoughts. Remember: Each signature step in your process should have a compelling learning sequence.

Imagine I'm creating a course called *Rewrite Your Financial Fairy Tale*. In the table on the following page, I've outlined a compelling learning sequence for one of my signature steps: Get real with your monthly expenses.

Course: Rewrite Your Financial Fairy Tale

Signature Step: Get real with your monthly expenses.

Content Area	Description	Ideas
Curiosity	Share a story, question, statistic, or quote.	Did you know that 85% of adults have no idea how much their monthly expenses are?
Understanding	Share any information that is required for action. What must they know to succeed?	• What is considered a monthly expense? • Where do I go to find out my monthly expenses? • How do I calculate an average of the last six months?
Action	State, specifically, what learners must do.	Now, it's time for you to get real with your monthly expenses. Your task: Complete the monthly expense worksheet.
Resistance	Respond to their "yeah, buts" before they even know they have them.	• "Yeah, but I don't have access to my bank statements." (Spend the next 30 days writing down every dollar you spend.) • "Yeah, but my partner and I share expenses." (Ask your partner to help you figure it out.) • "Yeah, but this sounds like a lot of work." (Is it more work than scrambling to break even every 30 days?)

Content Area	Description	Ideas
Vision	Ask them a question that brings them back to their "why."	Take a moment and consider: How would it feel to have money left over in your bank account at the end of the month? (Ask them to share in the chat or out loud)
Evaluation	Clarify success and recap the steps.	Your task: Complete the monthly expenses worksheet. Before our next class. You can download it here (add link)
Encouragement	Remind them they have everything they need to succeed.	Listen, I know this might feel scary. But I promise you, once you know what's happening with your money each month, you can create a realistic plan for a thriving future. I believe in you.

Course: _____

Signature Step: _____

Content Area	Description	Ideas
Curiosity	Share a story, question, statistic, or quote.	
Understanding	Share any information that is required for action. What must they know to succeed?	
Action	State, specifically, what learners must do.	
Resistance	Respond to their "yeah, buts" before they even know they have them.	

Content Area	Description	Ideas
Vision	Ask them a question that brings them back to their "why."	
Evaluation	Clarify success and recap the steps.	
Encouragement	Remind them they have everything they need to succeed.	

Create your second learning sequence.

Learning styles are like love languages. Are you familiar with love languages? Dr. Gary Chapman explains that we have five basic languages in which we give and receive love: words of affirmation, acts of service, gifts, quality time, and physical touch.

All that is great until the system breaks down. You see, each person has a preferred language to receive love. But, they tend to give love in that same language, and overlook the receiver's preference. Let's say my love language is gifts and yours is quality time. I've made sure your birthday present is unique and perfect.

What happens when you open your gift? You'll probably be thinking: If she really cared about our friendship, she would have taken me out for a long lunch.

Like love languages, most people design learning activities in their preferred style.

Let's say your preferred learning style is auditory, and you love listening to podcasts. You build an online group program full of narrated lessons. Yet, more than half your participants prefer a different learning style. How long will they stay engaged?

Not long. In this media rich world, video and audio are the norm. We often overlook the learners who need to engage in a conversation, ask questions, or apply the steps. One simple solution is to include an action step at the end of each lesson.

DAY EIGHT TASK

Create a compelling learning sequence for your second signature step.

Course: _____

Signature Step: _____

Content Area	Description	Ideas
Curiosity	Share a story, question, statistic, or quote.	
Understanding	Share any information that is required for action. What must they know to succeed?	
Action	State, specifically, what learners must do.	

Content Area	Description	Ideas
Resistance	Respond to their "yeah, buts" before they even know they have them.	
Vision	Ask them a question that brings them back to their "why."	
Evaluation	Clarify success and recap the steps.	
Encouragement	Remind them they have everything they need to succeed.	

Build your third learning sequence.

Do you ever get stuck in the "shoulds" of your business? The perfect lead magnet. A four sequence email welcome series. A how-to webinar to sell your premium product.

True confession: it happened to me recently. I was moving along and excited about my upcoming workshop. Then, bam. It hit me. I felt stuck. I was getting overly committed to the outcome. When this happens, I immediately ask myself three questions:

How can this be more me? If anything feels phony about what I'm creating, I won't follow through with sharing it. So I pause. I take a step back and think about what could bring to the project that would reflect who I am as a person and a creator.

How can this be more fun? When I'm having fun in my business, it feels like a playground or a day at the beach. When I'm having a great time, I seem to connect truly with my work and my network.

How can this be more useful? My purpose in my business is to contribute in meaningful ways. I enjoy creating tools that are directly related to a practical result or outcome.

Just in case you need a little boost to get you through your final learning sequence today, these questions might help. Oh, and your favorite playlist on repeat. That might help too!

Day 9 Task

Build a compelling learning sequence for your third signature step.

Course: _____

Signature Step: _____

Content Area	Description	Ideas
Curiosity	Share a story, question, statistic, or quote.	
Understanding	Share any information that is required for action. What must they know to succeed?	
Action	State, specifically, what learners must do.	

Content Area	Description	Ideas
Resistance	Respond to their "yeah, buts" before they even know they have them.	
Vision	Ask them a question that brings them back to their "why."	
Evaluation	Clarify success and recap the steps.	
Encouragement	Remind them they have everything they need to succeed.	

Gather your tools.

Now, it's time to gather the tools you'll need to facilitate your pilot and create your materials. Of course, these are my recommendations, but there are tons of options available. Let's look at all the tasks you'll need to accomplish:

SENDING EMAILS

A simple email marketing tool like Mailchimp is a good fit if you're just starting out building your email list. However, you can manage all of this using Gmail Groups if you'd prefer. Or, if you have an email marketing tool in place that you love and use already - stick with that one.

CREATING PRESENTATIONS

I love using Canva to create my training presentations! However, your favorite presentation tool, whether it's Powerpoint, Keynote, or Google Slides will work just fine.

BUILDING WORKBOOKS

I keep it simple and create my participant workbooks in Google Docs. This allows me to share them online, ask the learner to make a copy, and then they can take their own notes in their personal workbook. Especially for your pilot program, I recommend that you keep it simple. Now isn't the time to invest in a graphic designer.

DESIGNING A COURSE OVERVIEW

You'll need to create a simple course overview that is accessible online. Google Sites is entirely free. Mailchimp also has a landing page builder. I personally love using Squarespace. If you already know and use a web page design tool - keep with it! If not, I invite you to consider using an event management tool like Eventbright if you become overwhelmed when thinking about creating a web page.

COLLECTING REGISTRATION FEES

There are lots of entirely free and straightforward options to collect payments. Paypal is probably the most accessible and most familiar. However, Stripe is a payment processing tool that integrates with almost every other technology you'll use in the world of course creation. If you don't already have a Stripe account, I recommend that you take the time to set one up now. If you're using Mailchimp or Squarespace for your course overview page, you can integrate Stripe for a seamless payment process.

RECORDING LESSONS + TUTORIALS

I love the simplicity of Loom for recording lessons and tutorials. This tool makes life easy because you can simply share the link to your video without having to download, edit, then upload to a site like Youtube or Vimeo. Remember, for our pilot program, the goal is simplicity and effectiveness.

FACILITATING LIVE, ONLINE SESSIONS

Zoom is the leader in this area. I enjoy the ease of recording sessions, hosting them in the cloud, and easily sharing them with others. My workflow of whether I use Zoom or Loom depends on if I have live participants in the session. When I do, I use Zoom and record. When it's just me creating content, I use Loom.

DAY TEN TASK

Explore these tools and gather the ones you need for your course creation adventures.

Make decisions about the tools you'll use for each of the tasks above. Sign up for the services. Get your free trial. Play around a little. By the end of today, I hope you have your toolkit prepped and ready to go.

A quick note: You'll notice that one thing missing from this list is a learning platform. That's because I encourage every one of my clients to wait until after they have hosted a successful program to invest in these expensive, complicated tools. Your early success depends on it. If you can trust me on this one, I think you'll be glad you did.

Design your first lesson.

Let's do a quick review. You embarked on your course creation journey just 11 days ago. And now? You've selected the perfect (and most profitable!) topic, made a list of 5-10 ideal learners for your program, and set some revenue goals. You've also learned about your course creation style, written a clarity statement, and mapped your learner's transformation. You've got three compelling learning sequences ready to go and a belt full of tools. Whew! Take a deep breath and acknowledge what you've already accomplished!

Today, I'm going to share with you my nine-slide formula for designing course presentations that will make you think: "It can't be that simple." Believe me, it really is. This formula works. AND you're already prepped to follow it because you've designed your compelling learning sequences.

SLIDE 1

This is your title slide. It includes your course name, your name, the signature step you're teaching in this presentation, and a copyright notice.

SLIDE 2

On slide 2, use text and images to piques the curiosity you designed in your learning sequence.

- Sharing a story? Add an image that reminds you of what story to tell.
- Asking a question? Just some large type on a screen is pretty powerful.
- Presenting a statistic? Build a 50/50 screen with a number on one side of the slide and an image on the other.

- Sharing a quote? Insert a picture as a background, then place the text on top. Remember to add a filter, if needed.

SLIDES 3 + 4

Use these two slides to share the information your learners need to understand the action required for this step. Remember, you are the expert! You don't need to write every fact and process down on the slide. You only need a word or two that remind you what information to share and keep you on track. Learners will have the recording to go back to, if necessary, to get the details.

SLIDE 5

On slide 5, share the action that learners will take based on your signature step. Remember, as soon as they see this assignment, they will instantly encounter reasons why they are not ready to take this action yet.

SLIDE 6

On slide 6, you invite your learners to share every point of resistance they are feeling. Then, you guide them through it, offering ways to overcome the barriers. Offering encouragement of why they really are ready. Or strategies to succeed. Or acknowledging that it will require courage to take this step. On this slide, I like to include an image that conveys what participants are feeling but not saying (a sense of overwhelm, confusion, excitement.)

SLIDE 7

Bring them back to their vision. Remember the list of questions you answered about your ideal learner? The one where you listed out their big dream that they've rarely shared with anyone because it's so near and dear to their hearts? This is the time to prompt them to remember how good it will feel to make that dream come true. A question like: "Tell me. How will it feel when you have a six-figure course? How will your life be different?" A simple question and an image are all you need on this slide.

SLIDE 8

On this slide, tell participants exactly how to succeed. Share how they will evaluate themselves on the step. Let's say the signature step is to "Create a mood board for your business." On this step, you'll outline the details. "The mood board must either be online and shared with a link or uploaded as a photo. Your mood board must have at least 7 items on it. You must upload it by Friday at noon. I'll respond with feedback by Monday at 8 am." These specifics will comfort them when insecurity about their preparedness kicks in. They'll remember, "Oh yeah. I know exactly how to succeed here."

SLIDE 9

This is your final slide, and it's all about encouragement. With a simple image and verbal affirmation, remind participants that they have all they need to succeed. That you're here if they have any questions. And that you believe in them.

VOILA! That is the 9-slide sequence for a training presentation.

A quick note about teaching technical processes: Need to show someone how to do something in a program? It's much easier for you and your learners if you create a tutorial using Loom. Don't try to teach these types of tasks in your 9-slide sequence. Simply record a tutorial and let them know where they can watch it when they need to complete that specific task.

DAY ELEVEN TASK

Create your first 9-slide sequence in your favorite presentation tool.

Tip! Try not to get bogged down right now with picking the best, most beautiful template. Set a timer for 5 minutes and commit to using no more than that amount of time to select the one you'll use for this course.

Build your second lesson.

Let's talk about scripts for a few minutes. If you're a Workshop Wonder, you're probably not getting bogged down with scripting. But Mixed Media Mavericks and Focused Finishers tend to feel better about their progress in this portion of the course creation process when they have a nice, tidy script to work from.

Can I share a story with you? Year ago, I was presenting at a learning industry trade conference with a colleague. Joanna is most certainly a Focused Finisher! She dots her I's and crosses her T's every step of the way. In my attempts to match her style, I scripted my presentation word for word. I practiced presenting for the first time ever. And I proceeded to give the worst presentation ever, in front a room filled with my peers.

It was embarrassing! Not as awful as the time I fell running the 50-yard dash in front of the entire school in sixth grade, but that's a story for another time.

My point here is this: If scripting is not your thing and you're having a hard time figuring out what to share in your lessons, take a tip from one of my clients, Kaitlin. She loathed sitting down to create content, so we switched things up. Instead, I asked her to take a walk around her neighborhood, turn on her voice recorder, and describe her signature step as if she was teaching a class.

Then, she transcribed all her recordings to create her presentations and talking points.

DAY TWELVE TASK

Create your 9-slide presentation for your second signature step.

Create your third lesson.

Presentation design is personal. We all have a style that represents our personality. Yet, there are some general guidelines that can truly level up your learner's experience. Here's a recap of some of the best tips I've learned over the last 20 years as an instructional designer.

PHOTOS

Always take time to find high-quality images that evoke an emotion from your learner. One of my favorite places to find free photos online is Unsplash. Remember to credit the photographer.

SIMPLICITY

Have you ever gone on a quest to find the perfect image and looked up an hour later? Where did the time go?!? If this is you, I encourage you to keep it super simple for your lessons. Use a crisp white or black background with bold questions or phrases.

MORE SIMPLICITY

It's common as an expert that you appreciate other experts and want to share all that you've learned. Every process. Every framework. But I encourage you to limit yourself to one process or framework per signature step. Remember, your learners are looking for a path to transformation.

DAY THIRTEEN TASK

Create your 9-slide presentation for your third signature step.

Make some handy worksheets.

Worksheets are a great way to invite your learners to engage with the topics you're teaching. Here are five worksheet types to assist your learners in their transformation process.

The Reflection: Ask your learners to answer questions to help them reflect on the lesson.

The Analyzer: Provide your learners with a calculator or scorecard to measure outcomes.

The Tracker: Design a checklist to give your learners a sense of accomplishment with each step they take toward their goal.

The Planner: Give learners an action plan to map out their daily steps to success.

The Framework: Amplify a powerful concept by asking learners to adapt it to their own experience.

When it comes to creating your worksheet, there's not one best tool. Yet, over the years, I've found a favorite when it comes to your first iteration of your program.

I hope you'll consider keeping it simple and creating your worksheets in Google Docs. It's easy to share your worksheets with a simple link. Invite learners to "Make a Copy" and fill out each worksheet as the course progresses.

DAY FOURTEEN TASK

Create at least one worksheet for each of your signature steps.

Write your irresistible copy.

Think of the most recent course or program that you bought online. *Ask yourself: What compelled me to sign up?*

Your job today Is to transform your course into an irresistible offer. One that inspires visitors to take action, the same way you took action when you signed up for the course above. As you go through the steps in this task, keep the course page that hooked you open in one browser window. Recreate it using your own words, images, and brand in your platform. Use the language you can hear your ideal learner or customer using.

There are tons of statistics on "what works" and "what doesn't" for getting course registrations. Below you'll find content categories that help lead potential participants through their decision-making process. But what I've experienced and seen with my online programs is worth sharing here. The best way to attract your favorite clients is to be yourself. Have fun. Take a risk. Be silly. Or be serious. Be true to you.

A COMPELLING HEADLINE

Grab their attention, so they keep reading. Consider using a version of your course clarity statement.

AN OPENING STORY

Create empathy for the problem and the cost of not solving it.

BENEFITS OF THE TRANSFORMATION

Provide a simple list of 3-5 outcomes or course results. Consider a "what if" statement here...

YOUR AMAZING COURSE CONTENT

Describe each module or lesson and the included assignments. Pull these directly from your compelling learning sequences.

TESTIMONIALS

Convey social proof of your awesomeness as a professional. This can be two simple statements from happy clients not directly related to your course.

FAQs

Answer 3-5 questions about your course. Anticipate their hesitations and help them overcome barriers. (Typical objections include: I don't have time, I don't have the money, Now isn't the right time, etc.)

DETAILS

Create a placeholder to share dates, times, and links to register. You'll come back to this later in the process.

RISK REVERSAL

Share a guarantee to eliminate risk. (For example, if you're not completely happy with your investment 7 days into the course, I'll provide a full refund.)

POWER P.S.

Remind them of the cost of not signing up now. (Example: 30 days from now you could still be (unhappy, stuck, broke), or you could be (happy, moving forward, making money). Reassure them that your program will show them exactly how to achieve the transformation they seek.

DAY FIFTEEN TASK

Write irresistible copy that inspires people to register for your program.

And now, take a moment to think about what will be different in your life when you have a profitable course?

Make a commitment.

We already did some work with pricing when you calculated your ROI earlier in the process. But if you're still wrestling with pricing, here are three questions I ask to help me figure it out:

- What is the least amount of money you could make on your pilot and still feel valued?
- How much could you earn that would have you feeling delighted with your profits on this pilot?
- How much could you charge per person and still know that they will get three times that amount of value?

Now it's time to do a little math. Play with these numbers and see what feels right.

I had a client who designed her pilot as an intimate gathering of four existing community members. She made $10K on her pilot. Remember, anything is possible.

Day 16 Task: It's time to commit.

Let's face it, without a group of people waiting on you to share your brilliance - who value you enough to pay for it upfront - you might never finish your course.

Whether you have one person or ten people in your pilot isn't the point. Your pilot's purpose is to finish your course and finally begin to realize the actual value your expertise and experience is in the world.

So do it. Just do it. There's no magic date when everyone will be available. And there's no perfect time of year. Pick the dates and times that work for you. Then determine a price that will achieve profitability.

Go pull up your calendar and make it official. Seriously. Right now.

Don't keep reading until you've set your dates, times, and pricing.

If you're still hesitating, let me share this simple little statistic with you: 100% of my clients who finish their courses are profitable.

Are you ready to be a finisher?

Prepare to get paid.

Are you familiar with the term MVP? In the online business world, this doesn't refer to the Most Valuable Player (though I'm sure you are!). It stands for Minimum Viable Product. Here's a simple example:

Virgin Airlines is one of the largest British airlines operating internationally and is owned by Richard Branson. What was the minimum viable product for Virgin Airlines? It was just one route and one plane flying between Gatwick and Newark.

Think of your pilot as the MVP for your course. You're not making huge investments in technology or hiring a videographer to professionally record all your training videos at this stage. Instead, you're putting together a signature learning experience that creates a measurable transformation for your learners and achieves profitability. The goals are simple.

You'll amp up your technology once you prove your course works, and people are willing to invest in the transformation you are offering. Until then, we are keeping it simple.

Here are some options and considerations:

a) If you already sell products and services online through your store or website, use this same system for your course.
b) Leverage Stripe + Mailchimp to create a product on a landing page.
c) Use a simple Google Form to collect registration information and then email your learners a request for money using Paypal.

DAY SEVENTEEN TASK

Find a simple process for capturing registration information and collecting payments.

If you choose option A, create your product and save your link for your course overview page.

If you choose option B, set up both Stripe + Mailchimp, then integrate them. You'll set up your product when you design your landing page. (Tip! You can do all this with the free account.)

If you choose option C, create your Google Form to collect registration information. Confirm that your PayPal account is set up and working properly. Save the form link and add it to your course overview page in the next step.

I can feel the money coming your way!

Design an irresistible offer.

Think of your course overview page design as the presentation of your favorite dish on the plate. You know that your course is going to deliver the transformation you've promised. And you know you're creating a fantastic experience for your participants. But your job when designing your course overview page is to use design elements to convey credibility and excitement to your potential learner.

You've already written your copy (see Day 15). Today's task is to design your course overview page in a sharable format. That could be a simple PDF that you create using Canva, Word, or Google Docs. Or it could be an elaborate web page using your brand identity.

The complexity of the design isn't what's important. The goal here isn't to present a perfect course overview page. Focus your attention on finding images that convey the emotion you'd like for your participants to feel while completing your course.

Would you like for them to feel encouraged and calm? If so, add pictures that create that feeling for you. It's also a great idea to use some images of people that represent your ideal learner.

If you're hoping to work with heart-centered solopreneurs, then stay away from corporate images. Instead, choose photos of people working on their laptops outside or in a coffee shop.

Keep your fonts to a minimum. It's okay to use different fonts for your heading and body copy, but more than two fonts on a page will create a sense of chaos for your reader. I often use Unsplash to find high-quality free photos. Remember to credit the image if you do.

DAY EIGHTEEN TASK

Use your irresistible copy to design a page that brings in registrations.

Here's a list of five tools to consider using:

- Canva
- Mailchimp Landing Pages
- Google Sites
- Your Website
- Eventbrite

Once you've got your design pulled together, walk away. Come back to it a few hours later, and you'll see it with fresh eyes.

Craft the email invitation.

Sometimes the best way to teach is by example. Below, you'll find a beautiful example of one of the best email invitations to a pilot course that I've read. Chrisella Hertzog is a brand genius, and well...just read for yourself about her pilot program.

My comments are *{in brackets}.*

~~~~~~

A powerful brand is the foundation of a marketing strategy that leads to massive growth and revenue.

Through millions of dollars and decades of research, the biggest companies in the world have refined the art of branding into a science. They know how to create brands that build customer loyalty, and that creates an emotional connection between their customers and their products.

But the best branding minds in the world are out of reach for most small businesses. How will your company's branding compete with the millions of dollars thrown into corporate branding research every year?

{These first three paragraphs really establish a compelling purpose for Chrisella's course. As a small business, her ideal learners don't have millions of dollars to spend on branding, but they still need to compete.}

Over the past several years, I developed a process that brings all of the best branding knowledge together to help startups and small businesses. And now we're making this process even more accessible.

{In this paragraph, she's building credibility by sharing her process.}

I am so excited to invite you to join the beta program of the Brand Personality Bootcamp, a 6-week workshop where we dive deep into your company's values and voice, and give you the tools to communicate your brand message with courage and confidence.

{The invitation and course clarity message is delivered here, just in time.}

With the Brand Personality Bootcamp, you will be able to communicate your business message to your customers with ease, and you'll have the confidence and skills to adapt that message as your company grows. With every marketing touchpoint, you'll be able to show up with compelling, authentic marketing messages that allow the value of your services to shine.

{In these two paragraphs, Chrisella is highlighting the transformation learners' will achieve in her program and the positive impact it will have on their businesses.}

Our next cohort starts on October 13th and registration is limited to 12 people. Starting in 2021, the Brand Personality Bootcamp will only be offered once per quarter with a price tag of $1495. Because this is our beta run of this workshop, I'm offering this program at a massive discount. For this cohort only, the Brand Personality Bootcamp will be an investment of $495.

{Now, she effectively conveys details and demonstrates urgency with limited spots and a limited-time discount.}

If you're ready to join, you can find more details about the workshop and sign up here (http://humblehustle.studio/brand-personality-bootcamp)

Reserve your seat now!

Looking forward to working with you!
Chrisella Herzog
CEO, Humble & Hustle Studios

P.S. If the timing of this cohort doesn't work for you, but you still want to join, send me a message! We can make sure to save a space for you in a future cohort.

{And I love the way she's building her waitlist with this Power P.S.}

DAY NINETEEN TASK

Write a compelling email invitation to your program.

Here's a quick review of the key elements:

- Establish a compelling purpose and relevance for your course topic with your audience
- Build credibility in your experience and process
- Extend the invitation
- Recap the transformation, and why it matters
- Create urgency with timelines and discounts
- Provide a link to learn more and register
- Invite people to join a waitlist if the course timing isn't quite right for them

Reminder: While you are writing your email today, it's not time to send it yet. Keep it close by for an upcoming task.

Make a few notes about what you'll include in your email invitation.

Extend a warm welcome.

Once learners register for your program, you'll be doing a happy dance for sure! And guess what? So will they. Your program is the answer to the question they've been asking in their lives and businesses. Finally, they've found the guide they've been looking for to help make their big dreams come true!

So in this step, I encourage you to do a little something to boost that feeling for them. Your learners are investing in themselves - in their big dreams. That's a big deal.

This doesn't have to be elaborate or complicated. A personalized email will do the trick. On the following page you'll find a copy of my email welcoming learners into the Course Design Lab.

~~~~~~

I'm so excited you've decided to join the October cohort of the Course Design Lab!

As a little something to get you started, I'm sending over a workbook that will guide you through some planning steps for your course.

I know you already have a good idea about your topic, yet this process might clarify things.

You can download the workbook here (insert a link, of course!). Working through it before we get started will give you a jump start on success.

Please mark your calendar for the following dates + times:

- October 23 from 10 am - 4 pm ET
- October 27-29 from 2-3 pm ET

I'll send over calendar invitations in the next few days. I assure you that we'll have fun and take lots of breaks during our full lab day on the 23rd. Try to minimize distractions and be present as much as possible :)

Let me know if you have any questions! And I'll be in touch soon!

All the best,
Jeannie

P.S. Your special assignment! Send over your mailing address so that I can send a little surprise your way!

P.P.S. If you email me your completed workbook before we start class on the 23rd, I'll email you an exclusive bonus :)

DAY TWENTY TASK

Find a way to extend a warm welcome to your learners when they register for your program.

Here's a quick recap of the essential elements for your welcome email:

- Congrats, you took a big step today!
- Access and details: here's what you need to know.
- Ready to get started? Here's a little assignment to get you started.
- A signup surprise. I like to use Greetabl to put a little something in the mail. A handwritten card would be lovely as well!
- Access to an online community, if you have one. I choose to support my learners with a live call each month rather than an online community.
- Save the date information for any live sessions.

Remember, this step is focused on getting ready for your first registration. Simply draft it and keep it handy. You'll need it soon!

Design your referral program.

Once you launch your course, you only have two goals:

1. Make sure you do everything within your ability to bring about the transformation you promised your learners.
2. Give them an experience they can't help but share through your referral program.

Now, I know you've seen tons of referral programs online that use discount codes and tracking links. There's a time for setting all that up, but it's not right now. Right now, you need a simple way to say "thank you" when your learners refer your program to future learners.

Here are some ideas for you:

*   Ask on your registration form: Is there someone I can thank for sending you my way? Then send a handwritten thank you card.
*   Offer a $25 gift card for referrals. Ask participants to let you know when they've sent a new learner your way.
*   Gift exclusive services like 1:1 coaching to people who consistently refer others to your program.

When you lead a program that offers real transformation, the word gets out. However, a referral program can be a great way to keep your course sales rolling in without investing a lot of money in digital advertising. Your quest is to design a program and a referral system that reflects you - your values, goals, and priorities.

DAY TWENTY-ONE TASK

Design your referral program.

Create a simple handout and have it ready to share with participants about 3/4 of the way through your program.

Make some notes about compelling reasons to join your program.

Refine your learner experience.

"I've learned that people will forget what you said, people will forget what you did, but people will never forget how you made them feel." - Maya Angelou

Today, I want to ask you to take a hard look at what you've created so far. Ask and answer these questions. Be prepared to be brutally honest.

- What's missing from their experience?
- How could it be better?
- What could you add to make it more fun?
- What questions might they have that you haven't answered yet?

And the most important question of all: Have you designed a course you'd like to take?

If so, congratulations! I know you will be successful!

If not, kudos to you for being honest with yourself. Now, let's update your content and experience to make sure it IS a course you'd love to take and can be proud of!

DAY TWENTY-TWO TASK

Refine your learner experience.

Create a simple outline or map of the learner experience. It's helpful to go ahead and think of your ideal learner. Give them a name. For this example, we'll use Jordan.

- ✓ Jordan, who's already on the pilot program list of 5-10 people, receives a personalized email invitation to join your course.
- ✓ Jordan is excited and thinks: "Wow, this program is just what I've been looking for to help me accomplish my big goal this year!"
- ✓ Jordan accesses the Course Overview Page by either clicking a link in the email or opening up an attached PDF.
- ✓ Jordan reads through the course overview, thinking, "Wow, this course will help me overcome all the barriers I'm currently feeling. It's also offered at a discounted price just this time around. And I love trying new things. I'm in!"
- ✓ Jordan clicks on the Register Now button and pays the fees.
- ✓ Jordan stops for a second and wonders - did I make the right decision? Then, your welcome email arrives and calms Jordan's jitters.
- ✓ Jordan saves the live class dates, gets busy working on any prep assignments, and feels great about the investment.
- ✓ Jordan shows up to class and thinks: "Wow, this class isn't like any I've taken before. Instead of information overload, I'm feeling like I can actually do this."
- ✓ Jordan actually takes steps to create real transformation.
- ✓ Jordan is reassured that this course was worth it by answering the three magical questions (you'll learn about those later this week)
- ✓ Jordan is grateful, feels confident about the investment, can't stop talking about it, and refers friends your way.

Take time now to map out your learner experience. Tweak your process until you are genuinely excited to bring your first learner through the program.

Curate your bonuses.

Okay, now let's cover bonuses. You know, everybody likes a bonus. They help get people excited to invest in your program.

Here's what doesn't feel like a bonus: when your learners have to do more training. After completing the assigned curriculum, additional training modules tend to feel like work.

What templates do you use in your business? Do you have checklists you can share? What are the secrets that took you 10 years in business to uncover that you could share to save your learners precious time?

Any of these will make fantastic bonuses! If you don't have any of those to share (which I seriously doubt because I happen to know you're already an expert in your field), offer up some 1:1 time. Maybe even only to the first 3 or so people who register.

I really don't recommend creating more content at this point just for bonuses. If you don't have anything to repurpose, offer a bonus group Q+A session or something that you can just step right into, be yourself, and add tremendous value.

DAY TWENTY-THREE TASK

Compile your course bonuses.Here are some questions to help you along...

- ✓   What templates can you share?
- ✓   What checklists do you use?
- ✓   What's the secret to your success?
- ✓   How can you add 1:1 time to their experience?

Tip! You can add these bonuses to your course overview page or simply include them in the email invitation.

Write three magical questions.

"But how in the world do I differentiate my program in a saturated market?" I get this question in coffee chats all the time. And there's a clear answer everyone seems to overlook: RESULTS.

In a sea of online programs, which ones rise to the top? Which ones seem to fill themselves? The ones where participants are achieving the outcomes promised. I know what you're thinking: "But how do I do that?" Well, it's not easy, but it is simple.

What's easy is to resign yourself to being the information sharer. But you could choose to be the transformation guide. The consultants getting results combine learning design and coaching. They lead participants with a direct path of relevant content and accountability.

The good news is, you've already accomplished this by leveraging compelling learning sequences.

Today, your task is to create a system to measure the transformation that takes place during your program. This is quickly done by asking what I call the three magical questions.

These questions are magical for two reasons: First of all, answering them will help your learners get inspired to take action. Secondly, you'll gather the data you need to set your program apart as one that GETS RESULTS!

Ask these at the end of your program, not at the beginning or in the middle. Only at the end. And use a simple survey tool to gather your data. I like to use Google Forms because they make the Likert scale easy to use. (And, FREE!)

DAY TWENTY-FOUR TASK

Create a survey asking these three questions, customized to your course, of course.

Question #1
Before this course, how confident were you in your ability to _____ (insert course outcome). Responses include:

- Very confident
- Confident
- Somewhat confident
- Barely confident
- Not at all confident

Question #2
After this course, how confident were you in your ability to _____ (insert course outcome). Responses include:

- Very confident
- Confident
- Somewhat confident
- Barely confident
- Not at all confident

Question #3
How important is _____ (insert course outcome) to your overall success/happiness/fulfillment (choose most appropriate option for your course).

- Very important
- Important
- Somewhat important
- Not really important
- Not at all important

Be an encourager.

Once you're in the middle of teaching your course, you'll have a lot going on. Why not take 30 minutes today to draft a few encouraging emails for your learners. You can have these on the ready in a Google Doc so that when you're short on time, your learners can stay in the loop!

DAY TWENTY-FIVE TASK

Draft encouraging course emails.

Here's a list of emails to write now and remember to send during your program.

- ❏ Thanks for signing up!
- ❏ Class starts in just one week
- ❏ We're live tomorrow!
- ❏ Here's your recording + homework assignment
- ❏ Surprise bonuses like playlists or a fun picture or encouraging words
- ❏ Reminders for all follow-up classes
- ❏ Please answer three magical questions
- ❏ You did it! Course is completed!
- ❏ Join our referral program

Practice teaching.

I already know you're going to try to skip this task :) But if you've trusted me to get you this far along in the process, I hope you'll believe me when I say: THIS MAY BE THE MOST IMPORTANT TASK.

Please don't skip it. Do it for me. For you. For your future learners and the transformation you promised them.

Something spectacular happens when we go through this step in the Course Design Lab. In that context, I call these teach backs. Each participant spends 15 minutes teaching one lesson to the others in the lab.

Palms are sweaty, and stakes are high. These courageous learners are taking a risk by sharing their content with people who don't even match their ideal learner profile.

But every single time, the experience creates an unintended consequence: the facilitator realizes that the learning sequences work. Even in just 15-minute increments, transformation is possible, even with a group of people who wouldn't have signed up for the topic.

DAY TWENTY-SIX TASK

Practice teaching your lessons.

Use Zoom or Loom. Record yourself teaching. Go back and listen. Gather your kids or your mom or your best friend and ask them to be your learners.

I promise you'll be so glad you did this! In fact, if you do this step, send me an email: hi@jeanniesullivan.com with the subject line TEACHBACKS, YEAH! and let me know. I'll send you a little reward for being the courageous one.

Organize course materials.

Wow, can you believe you've made it this far? I sure can. I've believed in you all along. You wouldn't have picked up this book if you weren't ready to go for it.

Today is the day you gather up all you've created and put it in one place to make things easy for your learners. Typically, my clients get all worked up at this point and start looking into learning platforms.

Don't do it.

Not yet. You're not ready for that step or that price tag. Here's why: After your pilot, you're going to make some tweaks to your program.

That's great news! That's what pilot programs are for: to see what works and what doesn't. Up until now, you've taken your best shot at imagining what your learners will need to transform.

But I know you've missed something. Because you're the expert. Getting back into the beginner's mind is hard.

Don't beat yourself up about this! It happens every time.

Which is why I recommend that you don't spend a ton of time or hundreds of dollars setting up a learning platform right now. Keep it simple.

DAY TWENTY-SEVEN TASK

Organize access to your course materials.

1. Create a Dropbox or Google Drive folder.
2. Add your handouts, bonuses, and anything else your learners will need.
3. Upload your live, online class recordings here, too, after they are done.
4. Use this one link over and over again in the emails you send throughout the course.

I know what you're thinking: But what if they share the files with their friends? (You're thinking you need a learning platform to keep this from happening, right?)

Let me ask you a question: Have you ever shared your password with a friend so that they could watch a show on your Netflix account? A login and password act as a deterrent, but even they aren't a failproof solution.

So, also take these steps, for good measure:

- Put your name and copyright notice at the bottom of all your materials.
- Let your learners know that these materials were made exclusively for class participants.
- Reassure them that you are confident they'll respect your intellectual property by not sharing your content.
- Point them to your referral program.

Can you believe tomorrow is the big day? I'm excited too!

Press send on your invitations.

Hey! Guess what? You did it. You've created a course in just 28 days, and now it's time to move into profitability. And today, I'm going to give you a little pep talk, okay?

How many people do you know who have said they'd like to write a book one day? How many published authors do you actually know?

Thinking about creating a course and actually finishing one are two totally different things. And now you're about to take another giant leap! You're about to become profitable—a profitable course creator.

But there's one step left between you and profitability. You've got to invite people.

I know, I know. You wish the registrations would just roll in. And maybe you're scared that people won't like your course. Or that no one will register. Or that they'll roll their eyes when they see that email show up in their inbox.

Listen, courage is a muscle. And you must flex it daily if you want to succeed in the world of online business. Don't wait for the fear to go away; it won't. Trust me! I've waited. Sometimes years! Don't be like me. Be braver than me.

Know that if you've completed this process as I've outlined it, your course is already better than most programs out there. You've honed your process, eliminated the overwhelm, and created a signature experience. Today is the day.

DAY TWENTY-EIGHT TASK

Send email invitations to join your course to the 5-10 ideal learners on your list.

If you don't get any registrations right away, don't give up. Or say, "Oh, my course flopped." Instead, you send a follow-up email. Then, call them to see if they have any questions about the course.

If they simply aren't interested now or the timing isn't right, ask if they know anyone who might a great fit.

Then, you make a list of all your biggest fans who are also connectors. Call them. Tell them about your course and ask, "Would you be willing to share this with people you know who might benefit from it?"

Then, make a list of everything you think of to get five people in your pilot.

Call your grandma and ask her.
Send your dog out with a flyer.
Whatever you do, don't give up.

The world needs your course.

"I make lists to keep my anxiety level down." – Mary Roach

Step 1: Gather your learners.

Create a private community.
One of the first things you can do to reassure participants that they have made a great decision investing in your program is to give them a home base. This is your community. One free option is Facebook because it's an easy platform that everyone already knows - and doesn't require additional login steps.

Step 2: Give them a tour.

Create an overview map of your program.
Think of this as the map at the mall that says "You Are Here" next to the big red dot. This visual cue will allow your learners to see the expanse of the experience they are about to embark on. Also, they'll engage a visionary mindset that will prep them for their next step.

Step 3: Remind them of all the reasons why.

Create a welcome survey.
Your learners are primed with an overview of your learning program. Now, allow them to reconnect with why they've chosen to take this journey with you. Include these five questions:

- Why have you decided that NOW is the best time to make this change?
- What will be possible in your life or business after you've completed this transformation?
- What barriers do you foresee that could keep you from accomplishing your goals?

- How will you know when you've succeeded?
- What will success feel like?

Step 4: Give them a head start.

Create a quick start guide.
Most often, your learners share barriers that include: having enough time, managing priorities, and focusing on the assignments. Design your own quick start guide (less than 3 pages) with tips about time blocking, setting priorities, and creating accountability.

Idea! Why not send this to your learner in the confirmation email or screen after completing the survey in step 3?

Step 5: Unleash your gratitude.

Create a fantastic thank you page (or email!).
Now, it's time to pull it all together and create your learner's journey. This will require you to add a thank you page to your sales sequence.

Once they've clicked the last "register now" button and the funds have been transferred - redirect your newest learner to a custom thank you page. Here's an example of what to include there:

A thank you video expressing your genuine delight to have this learner in your program. Recognize her for investing in herself by signing up. You can do this using a free tool like Loom.

An invitation to head on over to the private course community lets her know that she will find a program overview once she arrives.

This is just the beginning.

Congratulations! You've created your course, hosted your pilot program, and now you're ready to transform your MVP into consistent learning-based revenue.

Here are some next steps that may be helpful.

REVIEW YOUR RESULTS

Remember the three magical questions? Gather your data. Analyze it. Then share your results on your course overview page for the next round of learners.

UPDATE YOUR CONTENT

Are there places in your course where learners needed more? Or perhaps you gave them too much information, and they became overwhelmed? If you're unsure of this question, invite 2-3 participants from your pilot to a short call and ask them to candidly share feedback on how you can improve the learning experience.

Keep in mind: You don't have to implement all of their suggestions. Simply receive the feedback, sleep on it, then ask: "What would I like to change, update, or edit to increase the odds of my learners realizing the transformation they seek?"

Now that you've analyzed your data to promote a proven online course and updated your content to amplify effectiveness, it's time for the next big step.

FILL YOUR COURSE

If I had a dime for every time someone has asked me: "What's the best way to market and sell your online course?" Well, I'd definitely be on vacation right now.

There's no simple answer to this question. Yet, there are some guidelines I'd like to share to help you think through what will work best for you and your course.

First, answer this question:

Is the ideal learner for your course the same as the person you serve with your existing services? If so, fold your course sales into your current business development process.

For example, let's say you have a discovery call with a new prospect. You'd enjoy working with this individual, and you think you can help. But their budget isn't quite big enough for your individual services.

Invite them to join your online course. Voila!

What if the ideal learner for your course isn't in the same audience as your existing services?

You'll want to create a separate invitation strategy. It starts with what I call a "meet-cute." You may know this term from romantic comedies (which I love!). It's the moment when two people connect serendipitously, and sparks fly.

Meet your future participants at the perfect time with a helpful quiz or checklist. Then, share useful information via email over the next week or so. Do this in the most authentic way possible - with a genuine desire to help, not sell.

Then, invite them to join your program. Perhaps offer an exclusive discount or ask readers to join a Q+A session to learn more about your course. The goal is this: CONNECT + INVITE.

EVERGREEN PROGRAMS

I'd also like to share with you a little note about evergreen programs. The good and bad news is that while online learning is still growing as an industry, the one category of training that isn't thriving is the self-directed online course.

It's easy to see why this is happening. Learners are growing weary of spending money on courses they never complete or that don't deliver. If you've followed the steps in this book, your program doesn't fall into this category. You've designed a path to guide learners directly to the transformation they are after.

An easy way to overcome this barrier to evergreen success is to integrate an accelerator program within your self-directed online program. An accelerator program combines the self-study content with a live, online facilitator-led accountability and support program.

If you haven't yet taken Gretchen Rubin's quiz on the Four Tendencies, I hope you will. Keep in mind that the majority of your course participants fall into the category she calls Obligers. They require external accountability to meet both inner and outer expectations.

Look for ways to build this accountability into both your self-directed format and your accelerator program.

And here's a hint! If you completed the process in this book, chances are excellent that you are NOT an obliger. How do I know? You finished this program on your own.

If you're feeling frustrated because you truly desire to create a course, but you didn't finish this process, there's nothing wrong with you. You're probably an obliger, my friend. And the great news about being an obliger is that it's super easy to set up external accountability to achieve your biggest dreams!

If you've tried to create a course using this book, but you'd like a little more structure, I invite you to check out my live, online program, the Course Design Lab. You can learn more here: jeanniesullivan.com/lab.

ACKNOWLEDGEMENTS

"Dreaming, after all, is a form of planning." - Gloria Steinem

Thank you, Rollins, for always dreaming with me, even when you knew that most of my big ideas would never become a reality. And of course, for lying in the driveway and counting the stars.

Sully, your own commitment to creating the life you want, your way, is a constant reminder to me that anything is possible. You came into this world, knowing who you are. Thank you for being patient with me while I figure it out.

And Brian, your consistent and gracious encouragement to be me is a gift I'd never felt worthy of asking for.

Finally, thank you, Christi Byerly! You have shown up repeatedly in my life to reflect back to me the beautiful ways the content of this book has impacted your life. And through your work, it continues to make a difference in others' lives by your courageous willingness to teach.

ABOUT THE AUTHOR

"The privilege of a lifetime is being who you are." - Joseph Campbell

Jeannie Sullivan is a business coach and learning strategist. Right after graduate school, she fell in love with the field of instructional design. Working with Fortune 500 companies, Jeannie had the chance to solve problems, launch big ideas, and inspire adults to take action, all under the guise of building training programs. A few years later, she became a certified professional coach. Since saying goodbye to corporate America in 2010, Jeannie has coached 200+ professionals. She provides guidance on becoming better leaders, leaving corporate jobs to become solopreneurs, and designing profitable learning-based revenue streams. Jeannie has also created training programs for many Fortune 100 companies on Customer Service, Sales Performance, and Women in Leadership. When she's not creating training programs or working with clients, you can find Jeannie paddle boarding on Lake Murray or baking chocolate chip cookies.

If you'd like to learn more about creating courses, visit Jeannie's website: jeanniesullivan.com

If you'd like to download free resources to enhance your course creation experience, sign up here: jeanniesullivan.com/28days

Printed in Great Britain
by Amazon